790

DATE DUE

DEC 2 1 1981			

Walter, Claire
  Women in sports: skiing

WOMEN IN SPORTS

SKIING

by Claire Walter

Illustrated with photographs

Harvey House, Publishers
New York, New York

ACKNOWLEDGEMENTS FOR PHOTOGRAPHS:
Bausch & Lomb Council on Sports Vision 1, 29
Joanne Dearcopp 5
Foto Sundhofer 7, 9, 10, 12
Stan Phaneuf 18
Eastern Ski Association 19
Swiss National Tourist Office 24, 33
Barry Stott, Compliments of the Colgate World
 Trophy Women's Freestyle Ski Tour 25, 27, 28
Canadian Mountain Holidays 30
Greater Reno Chamber of Commerce 31
Giuseppe Ghedina 35
Telluride Corporation 36

To my parents Oscar and Louise Walter who
encouraged me to ski and to my husband Burns
E. Cameron who encouraged me to write about it.

Library of Congress Catalog Card Number 77-80616
Manufactured in the United States of America
ISBN 0-8178-5612-9

Published in Canada by Fitzhenry & Whiteside, Ltd., Toronto

Harvey House, Publishers
20 Waterside Plaza
New York, New York 10010

CONTENTS

FOREWORD

Women's international ski races are every bit as exciting as men's events. Most major international meets are held in Europe, and the most important of these are grouped together in a season-long circuit called the World Cup. The greatest honor for a skier is winning the World Cup combined at the end of a racing season, or just placing well in the standings.

Skiers compete in three races: The slalom is a fairly short race with many turns down a steep hill. Each skier makes two runs, and the results are based on combined time. The giant slalom is longer and contains fewer turns. The downhill is the longest, fastest and most exciting. Each skier makes one run in the giant slalom and downhill. Times are reckoned in hundredths of seconds.

The Olympic Games, held every four years, are the best known ski competitions. In 1948 at St. Moritz, Switzerland, Gretchen Fraser won a gold medal, starting a tradition of which American women can be very proud. Of the 14 gold, silver and bronze medals won by U.S. skiers, 12 have been won by women.

There are also professional ski events for women. Three professional races have been held in recent years, but the big attention — and the big prize money available — has been in freestyle skiing.

Most of the skiers described in this book started skiing when they were very young, and they are among the best women skiers in the world. They have one attribute in common: individual determination to excel in the highly competitive and demanding sport of ski racing.

ONE The Golden Lollipop: Barbara Anne Cochran

Barbara Ann Cochran can't remember a time when she didn't ski. She grew up in a mountain town in Vermont during the 1950's and was racing on skis before most children enter grade school. Then Barbara Ann competed in ski races to win lollipops! Fifteen years later, she achieved her greatest skiing triumph — she won a gold medal in the 1972 Winter Olympics.

Barbara Ann Cochran comes from a skiing family. There are four Cochran children and each of them began skiing before they were five years old! Marilyn, the oldest, skied excellently from the beginning. Barbara Ann and Bobby, the next two, followed in her ski tracks, and Lindy, the youngest, learned fast and soon was keeping up with her older sisters and brother.

The father of these young skiers, Mickey Cochran, had always been fascinated by ski racing, and his fascination strongly influenced his children's lives. While Marilyn, Barbara Ann, Bobby and Lindy were first learning how to ski, Mickey loved to spend long hours coaching them and other children who took part in lollipop races and other ski competitions. He moved the family to Vermont

9

when Barbara Ann was five years old and built a ski tow on the hill behind the Cochrans' house. He bought some wooden poles, placed them in pairs on the hill, and encouraged his children and their friends to practice slalom skiing every chance they could. Mickey was an engineer, so he used great precision in creating his ski course and in measuring the exact places on the course where skiers should make their turns. He helped every young skier pick the best route through the forest of poles he had set, and he kept on stressing speed and efficiency.

Mickey's coaching paid off. By the time Marilyn was 20 and Lindy was 17, the three oldest Cochrans were on the A-squad of the U.S. Ski Team and young Lindy was on the B-team, the country's second-ranked racing team! For one family, that was an amazing achievement.

From their earliest years on skis, the racing Cochrans had to stay in top physical condition to keep up with their demanding race schedules and their school work. Each June, they headed for mountain areas where there was still snow so they could keep on practicing. If they didn't visit Mt. Hood, Oregon, or Red Lodge, Montana, they travelled to Portillo, Chile, where winter takes place during our summer months. Sometimes they would spend a few weeks training on glaciers high in the Austrian and Italian Alps.

After their summer practice sessions, the Cochrans usually headed home for a few weeks of school and intensive physical fitness training with their father. When United States skiing started again each November, they joined their teammates and went to training sessions all over the country. Whenever they were on the road like this, their school work took the form of independent study assignments.

The 1969-1970 ski season was the first in which there

were three Cochrans in international races. Marilyn won a World Cup slalom, Barbara Ann took second place in the 1970 World Championship slalom, and brother Bob was considered to be the best American downhiller of the season.

The Cochran family first captured the imagination of the ski world in 1970 at the World Championships at Val Gardena, Italy. While only the top three skiers in any event of this competition receive medals, finishing in the top ten is a great accomplishment because usually only split seconds separate the first and tenth place finishers. Three American women had top-ten placings at Val Gardena: Marilyn and Barbara Ann Cochran, and their teammate Judy Nagel. Only one American male skier, Billy Kidd, placed in the top ten.

A salute to the Cochran family by the town of Richmond, Vermont, in April 1969.

**The Cochran ski team (left to right): Lindy, age
10 and Barbara Ann, age 13.**

By 1972, the three oldest Cochran skiers were members
of the U.S. Ski Team and were competing in the Winter
Olympics in Sapporo, Japan. The team was not doing
very well. Susie Corrock, a bubbly twenty-year-old from
Idaho, had succeeded in winning a bronze medal in the
downhill, but her teammates — especially the men —
were not up to form. Barbara Ann, a top slalom skier,
became the U.S. team's only hope for a gold medal.

Pressures on Barbara Ann increased as the Olympics
continued. No one worried about her training or her ability, but many worried that the disappointing performances of her brother and sister had discouraged her.

Barbara Ann, petite, blond, and very much alone, knew
that everyone — her family, her team, and her country
— was counting on her. Like a true champion, she tried
to ignore the stress and concentrate on her skiing. "I
knew a lot of pressure was on me," she said later, "but
I kept telling myself that the Olympics was just another

race. It demanded nothing of me that I hadn't done before. I had to use the same skills in Sapporo that I had used in every other race I'd ever entered."

The night before the slalom event, Barbara Ann broke an Olympic Village rule by going to the boys' dormitory to see her brother. Bob's last-minute encouragement boosted Barbara Ann's morale, and she remembered all the years of hard work that had gone into getting ready for this very important race. The next day, she felt more at ease as she took the ski lift up Mt. Teine and joined her competitors.

Barbara Ann was the first skier out of the starting gate in the first of two runs. She skied smoothly, snaking her skis through the gates and pressing for time at every turn. When all the racers had completed their first run, Barbara Ann was just three one-hundredths of a second ahead of second-place Daniele Débernard of France.

In the second run, the starting order was reversed and the number of starters was reduced by the women who had been disqualified because of falling or missing a gate. Ten skiers negotiated the tricky course again before Barbara Ann took her last turn at the starting gate.

Snow was falling in big heavy flakes, and visibility was almost zero. Everyone was tense. How could Barbara Ann, the "Final U.S. hope," turn in a winning run in almost blizzard conditions? Daniele Débernard had clocked an extremely good time — 45.18 seconds — for her second run, giving her a combined time of 91.26 seconds. Barbara Ann's time for the second run would have to be 45.20 seconds or less in order to hold her lead. She had a chance for the gold medal — but only if she didn't make a single mistake!

Her run was smooth and fast. She streaked past tele-

Victorious Barbara Ann carried by her brother Bob and her friend Rick Chaffee after winning the gold medal for slalom in Sapporo, Japan.

vision cameras and thousands of spectators, ignoring the swirling snow and thinking only of the clock. She hurtled through the finish line and stopped short in front of the scoreboard. Before she could catch her breath, her brother Bob and teammate Rick Chaffee broke through the crowd and hoisted her onto their shoulders. The clock read 45.19 — she had won the Olympic gold medal by two one-hundredths of a second!

How do you follow such a triumph if you're a skier? If your name is Barbara Ann Cochran, you keep on racing. While many others would have retired after hitting the top, Barbara wasn't ready to quit.

The 1972-73 season wasn't one of Barbara's best, even though she had many high point placings in World Cup competition. The stress of world travel was catching up with her. Overworked and exhausted, she contracted mononucleosis and could not compete again until the following season.

In 1973, Mickey Cochran was named coach of the U.S. Ski Team — another Cochran family triumph. With five talented Cochrans on one team, sports experts were predicting a winning season for the United States. Unfortunately, a disagreement began between Mickey and several team officials. Mickey wanted to spend most of his time working with his skiers and coaching them in all of their practice sessions. The officials wanted him to get more involved in fundraising activities. The difference of opinion couldn't be resolved, so Mickey quit.

Mid-season coaching changes hurt any team, and the U.S. Ski Team was no exception. Early in the season, Barbara Ann and Lindy had each won a silver medal in World Cup races, but by March, when the 1974 World Championships were starting, the American team was not in winning form. Barbara Ann's seventh place finish in

the giant slalom was the best American score of the meet. She ended the year by placing seventh in the season-long World Cup point total in the slalom, the best American placing in a disappointing year.

Barbara Ann Cochran stopped competing in World Cup races in the spring of 1974. She resumed her studies in home economics at the University of Vermont and took on coaching duties with the University's ski team.

During her free time, Barbara Ann competed in a professional ski event, the Hang Ten Competition, to race for money instead of medals. In 1975, she won the Hang Ten slalom race at Hunter Mountain, New York, proving that she was still one of the best slalom specialists around. In the 1976 Hang Ten, she took fourth place because of an unlucky spill during an excellent run.

Today, as this book is being written, women's professional ski racing is stagnating. Only one professional women's event — the Hang Ten — ever took place. Even though women athletes found it difficult and frustrating to train for only one event a year, at least they **had** an event. Now they have none, despite the fact that there are dozens of professional competitions for male skiers.

When and if women's professional racing begins again, Barbara Ann Cochran and her skiing sisters will probably be right there — racing not for lollipops, but for cash.

TWO World Cup Comeback: Anne Marie Moser-Proell

No woman skier is better known in Europe than Annemarie Moser-Proell, the Austrian who won her fifth straight World Cup title in the 1974-75 ski season. No other skier, man or woman, has won **five** World Cups! Many people call her the best woman racer of all time because of that incredible record.

Annemarie was a natural ski racer from the very beginning, demonstrating both the power and the determination to do well. Skiing is very important to the Austrian national economy. The government subsidizes its ski team so that its top skiers can make the sport their primary concern. This means that Annemarie always had the benefit of the best training and equipment that Austria could offer.

Annemarie burst upon the international ski scene in 1969 by placing second in a World Cup downhill at St. Gervais, France. She was only 15 years old, but she earned 18th place in the total World Cup standings. The next season, she finished in seventh place, and in 1971 she won her first World Cup.

She began to earn the reputation of being a strong-minded, stubborn skier who insisted on doing things her own way. Whenever she made her mind up about anything, not even her coaches or ski officials could change it. Throughout her racing career, Annemarie was one of the few skiers who broke training rules by smoking. Her coaches didn't approve and told her so, but Annemarie kept smoking. She knew it was unhealthy, but she also knew that quitting took a lot of hard work. She decided she would rather pour all that extra energy into skiing faster than into breaking the smoking habit. She did so well in her races that no one ever forced her to quit.

Annemarie earned another World Cup during the 1971-72 season and wanted very much to win an Olympic gold medal. But the 1972 Austrian ski team did very poorly at the Winter Olympics in Sapporo, Japan. Team members were upset because Olympic officials had banned their best male skier — Karl Schranz — from competing because they said he was no longer an amateur. Amid all of this excitement, Annemarie was able to win two silver medals for Austria in the downhill and giant slalom. But she regarded these as "defeats" because all that ever mattered to her in racing was top place.

After the disappointment at Sapporo, Annemarie made a strong comeback by winning all eight downhill races of the 1972-73 ski season. It began to seem like she was unbeatable in the downhill and barely beatable in the giant slalom. Reporters began to swarm around her everywhere she went, but Annemarie was becoming just as famous for ducking interviews as she was for winning races. She felt it was better to be modest than to brag because she might "hit a low in the next race."

Then, at the age of 20, she married a 28-year-old soccer player named Herbert Moser, and the European ski world buzzed with rumors that she would quit her racing career.

Annemarie enjoyed proving her critics wrong. "Why shouldn't I bring my record of World Cup victories up to four?" asked the skiing bride, and she kept on racing. The name Moser-Proell began to head the victory lists as Proell had done before. At the end of the winter, with the Cup assured, she turned in the best slalom performance of her career by tying for first place in the first of two runs at Mont Ste. Anne, Quebec.

The following season opened with more victories for Annemarie, and they were becoming so numerous that it was hard to remember them all. She was finally beaten for the first time in 1974 by a young, little-known American named Cindy Nelson. More gracious in defeat than she usually was in victory, Annemarie explained simply: "Cindy Nelson just skied better than I did."

A week later, she achieved a tremendous 2.5 second victory in a downhill race against Switzerland's Marie-Thères Nadig, who had beaten her in both the downhill and the giant slalom at Sapporo two years earlier.

In February, she competed in the World Championships at St. Moritz, Switzerland. The first race was the woman's giant slalom. Marie-Thères Nadig hoped to repeat her Olympic triumph, but pressures became too much for her and she disqualified. Annemarie skied strongly and posted a lead time of 1:44.24, but she was overtaken by the next woman skier on the course, radiant Fabienne Serrat of France, who shaved more than a second off Annemarie's time. In the end, Annemarie was out of the medal running, nosed out by West Germany's Traudl

Annemarie and her sister Evi Proell.

Treichl for a silver and France's Jacqueline Rouvier for a bronze.

The next race was the downhill, Annemarie's specialty. She exploded out of the starting gate and drew on her incomparable strength to finish the rough course in 1:50.84. No other skier came close. The runnerup, Betsy Clifford of Canada, was more than a second behind her.

Slalom had never been a strong event for Annemarie, but she decided to give it her greatest try at St. Moritz. Instead of playing safe and aiming for a top ten placing which would assure her of a gold medal in the combined, she skied like a demon, pressing for time at every gate. The pace and the course proved too tough for her, and she disqualified. Although she had earned gold and silver medals in individual races, she was disappointed because she had no standing in the combined.

In the autumn of 1974, a new head coach was assigned to the Austrian women's team. That year, the team consisted of highly experienced racers like Annemarie, Monika Kaserer, Wiltrud Drexel and Ingrid Gfoelner. They had made the Austrian women's team the best in the world for several seasons, but now they began to complain. They felt that the new coach was treating them like raw recruits and that he wasn't capable of teaching them anything about racing that they didn't already know. They threatened to skip training if officials did not replace him. Such a "strike" could easily ruin Austria's chances for victory in any competition.

Annemarie had a reputation for being temperamental and for not speaking up for anyone but herself. Yet she suddenly found herself the leader of her team's protest.

She negotiated a compromise with the Austrian ski officials and a new coach who was more capable and understanding was appointed. "Everything is going well now," Annemarie told surprised reporters after it became known that **she** had been the peacemaker. "We have learned to laugh again and we're getting fun out of our training." The European press, which had always criticized her blunt and outspoken manner, now praised her for her diplomacy.

Annemarie's winning pace slowed down a little that year. Some people said it was because she was becoming bored. She was winning many races, to be sure, but her non-winning placings were lower than usual. Even before the 1975 New Year was rung in, European fans speculated that Annemarie was about to retire.

The only skiing honor left for Annemarie Moser-Proell was the Olympic gold medal, and 1976 would have to be the year for her to win it. But she started making noises about her retirement, and Austrian fans began to worry because without her, her country had little chance for a gold medal. As the weeks passed, Annemarie did not make one move toward preparing for the Olympics. When the 1975-76 international season opened, Annemarie's younger sister, Evi, was in the starting gate for Austria. The five-time World Cup winner had indeed retired, and she attended the Winter Olympics at Innsbruck as a commentator for an Austrian newspaper.

But a year off was enough for the restless Annemarie. As suddenly as she had retired two seasons before, she "unretired" at the start of the 1976-77 ski season, ready to become the first skier to attempt a World Cup comeback. Always capable of amazing physical feats on skis, Annemarie raced less than a month after undergoing emergency surgery and placed third in the first race of the season — a giant slalom held in a blinding snowstorm at Val D'Isère, France. She then achieved her first comeback win on a demanding downhill run at Cortina d'Ampezzo, Italy.

Annemarie broke out of the starting gate, pushed herself as hard as she could, and was near tears from the effort. She crossed the finish line with a time of 1:34.43, winning her first race in 20 months by a 1.5 second margin.

More high placings followed, but the World Cup was not the "sure thing" that it had been for her when she was younger. In the past, her point margins had always been so overwhelming that she consistently clinched the World Cup by mid-season. The only suspense that remained for fans during those years was the speculation over who would earn **second** place. But this was not the case in her comeback season.

Lise-Marie Morerod, a slalom specialist from Switzerland, was piling up impressive World Cup points and was viewed as Annemarie's strongest rival for the overall title. The World Cup lead seesawed back and forth between them. Annemarie, who had trained hard for the competition, was winning the lion's share of the downhills, through with smaller margins than in her preretirement years. Her rival was picking up many slalom points. Aware of Annemarie's strong will, Lise-Marie skied as skillfully as she could and observed: "Annemarie has as much determination as **two** champions combined."

In January 1977, Lise-Marie took a definite lead, and in February she looked like she was clinching the title . With most of the downhills out of the way, Annemarie appeared to be out of the running for her sixth World

Cup. Lise-Marie had earned the giant slalom and slalom titles and was comfortably ahead in the overall.

The year's last downhill World Cup competition took place at Heavenly Valley, California. At the start of the race, Annemarie's hopes were already gone for capturing the overall title, but she was leading in downhill points and was expected to capture the downhill championship. Instead, she was defeated by her longtime teammate Brigitte Habsersatter-Totschnig on a flat, easy course. Brigitte edged ahead of Annemarie in the downhill standings and Lise-Marie took the overall title. Brigitte was elated, Lise-Marie was thrilled, but Annemarie could only leave the awards area to be alone with her tears. She had finished her comeback season with second place in the downhill and second overall. For any other racer, that would have meant a triumphant return and a triumphant year. For Annemarie, the all-time champion of the sport, it was defeat.

At the end of the season no one — probably not even Annemarie Moser-Proell herself — knew whether she would race again in 1977-78.

THREE The Lutsen Bomber: Cindy Nelson

Cindy Nelson was first put on skis when she was two. Her mother, a ski instructor, had put her two other children, George and Becky, on tiny skis when they were young and had encouraged them to slide and walk with them as they played in the snow. Cindy received the same basic training, and as an "old lady" of three, she began to ski in earnest.

When Cindy was almost six, her mother thought her three young skiers would enjoy entering a children's race at the Nelson's Lutsen ski area in Minnesota. That day, George and Becky took off from the starting gate and ably navigated the brightly colored slalom poles on the hill. When Cindy's turn came, she asked her mother what she should do. "Just ski between poles that are the same color till you get to the bottom," her mother explained. She did, and although Cindy the tot didn't make any great mark on the Midwestern racing scene that day, she **did** show a tremendous liking for competition.

By the time Cindy was 11, she had skied between thousands of same-color poles and was showing great skiing promise. When she was 15, she fulfilled part of that promise by qualifying for the 1971 Junior National Championships at Mammoth Mountain, California. That was her first step toward the big time and a place on the U.S. Ski Team.

Seasons of downhill training on high mountains, at racing camps and in national championships soon taught Cindy the important role that high speed plays in competition. As a youngster, she was slightly afraid of such speeds. An unpleasant and frightening experience on a steep slope helped her overcome her fear for good.

**Eight year old Cindy skiing at her parents'
ski resort in Lutsen, Minnesota.**

Cindy's mother giving her encouragement before the Junior National.

At a camp at Mt. Bachelor, Oregon, Cindy hit a bump on a downhill course, was thrown forward dozens of feet, and landed between two large pine trees. She wasn't hurt, but her skis had broken. She borrowed another pair, but found that she was too shaken to ski again that day. Fear prevented her from skiing the next day and the next, but some heavy thinking made her realize that she was running away from a necessary technique that she **had** to have to compete with the best. Cindy wanted to **be** the best as well as compete with the best, so she decided to ski again. Her confidence in herself and her ability as a skier was never shaken again.

In December 1971 Cindy won three out of four downhill time-trial races and was named to fill an unexpected vacancy on the U.S. Ski Team. This was an exciting promo-

29

tion because the 1972 Winter Olympics were right around the corner. Cindy was eager to go to Sapporo and race against the finest women skiers in the world, and she began to train very hard to earn her place as the youngest skier on the U.S. squad. During the early months of 1972, she placed 12th and 13th in the downhills at Val d'Isère and St. Moritz, excellent placings for a newcomer on the World Cup circuit.

But the thrill of racing in the 1972 Olympics was not in the cards for Cindy. In the last pre-Olympic downhill race at Grindelwald, Switzerland, she took a bad fall and dislocated her hip. She was out of competition for the rest of the season.

Cindy's hopes were high for the upcoming 1972-73 ski season. Her placings before her injury had assured her of a start in the first seed of the downhill, meaning she would be among the first 15 out of the starting gate in all the World Cup downhills. She was one of seven young women training at Stratton Mountain, Vermont, before the team was scheduled to go to Europe. Suddenly, the coaches announced that only **five** skiers would be able to go because of a lack of funds. Cindy was one of the two ordered to stay home.

In a similar situation, some skiers on the men's team had paid their way to Europe to join the World Cup circuit. But ski association officials couldn't decide whether to allow Cindy and her friend Susie Patterson to do the same thing. The two girls were left behind, but they soon scrounged up enough money for air fare to Europe.

Cindy and Susie were happily reunited with their teammates at Maribor, Yugoslavia. They showed up for the slalom, skis waxed and ready to race. But coach Tom Kelly told them they wouldn't be able to compete. If **they** raced, Kelly explained, the U.S. Ski Association felt it would have to allow **any** skier who could come up with travel money to compete.

Cindy was put on the Can-Am circuit, which is like a mini-World Cup series for United States and Canadian racers. She was disappointed and almost was tempted to quit racing. But she got her determination back and put everything she had into this new competition.

She started the Can-Am races well by winning a slalom and by placing third in a downhill. As she won more and more races, her spirits soared. She won the Can-Am downhill trophy for the season and placed second in the combined.

Cindy Nelson was back on the U.S. Team in 1973-74 on the strength of her Can-Am showings. She started the New Year of 1974 by placing sixth in the World Cup downhill at Pfronten, Germany.

The next downhill was at Grindelwald, where Cindy had injured her hip before the 1972 Olympics. Rosi Mittermaier of West Germany posted a strong time down the difficult course and took the lead. Cindy was the fifth racer to start. At the midpoint, her time was excellent. Her technically refined downhill turns held her through a difficult chute-like bend about 500 feet above the finish line. Cindy Nelson pushed into first place.

Annemarie Proell was eight racers behind Cindy. At the midpoint of her run, her time was 36/100 of a second slower than Cindy's. She had been behind by more than that in past races and had won with ease. But on January 13, wearing number 13, Annemarie was bested by an 18-year-old American named Cindy Nelson by a mere 7/100 of a second.

Now Cindy hit a hot streak. At Les Diablerets, Switzerland, three days later, the downhiller proved she was no

The Nelson sisters: Cindy, Terri, and Traci.

one-event skier. She came in fifth in the slalom and earned her first World Cup points in that event.

A week later, Annemarie was back in top form, winning the downhill at Badgastein, Austria, by 2.4 seconds. Cindy was seventh. When asked by a reporter what had gone wrong, she answered: "There was nothing wrong with the course, but I had trouble relaxing in the flats." Was she satisfied with her performance? "Nothing is as satisfying as winning," said Cindy.

She didn't perform as well as she had hoped at the World Championships at St. Moritz, finishing eleventh in the downhill. But then, it was a disappointing competition for the entire U.S. team. The racer from Lutsen finished the European season in fourth place in World Cup downhill standings, the best rating for any American woman ever.

In June the U.S. team skied at Mt. Hood, Oregon. In July, there was a specialized high-altitude training program at Aspen, Colorado. In the thin air 8,000 feet above sea level, Cindy's program included such rigorous activities as long-distance and sprint running, weight lifting, agility training, and cycling.

With that great training under their belts, the team members headed for Portillo, because winter in Chile falls in August and the mountain area would have plenty of snow.

Cindy had had an injury-free season, a string of high placings, and had gone through a long period of tough conditioning. Her form and her spirits were in great shape, and now, at Portillo, she was receiving the finest downhill training of her career. Women skiers were training with men skiers, and both squads were pushing for extremely high speeds. Skiing against the men, who are stronger and heavier and therefore faster, forced Cindy to achieve higher speeds.

The 1974-75 season started with a slowed-down Annemarie Moser-Proell coming in seventh in the first downhill. Annemarie shrugged off her critics by saying: "I had a very good race." Now that Cindy was also a veteran of the World Cup circuit, she could act just as cool as Annemarie. When complimented about her fourth-place finish, she smiled and said she wasn't surprised at her good performance. By this time she knew that World Cup was no junior competition and that fourth place was very good indeed, especially for accumulating World Cup points.

Cindy's next World Cup placing was second in the downhill at Cortina, Italy, which netted her points **and** a silver medal. Saalbach, Austria, was the scene of the next downhill, and Cindy was really ready for it. The course was long and had the fast turns and straightaways that Cindy liked. She made up her mind that she would either win or push herself so hard that she would fall. There would be no second place for Cindy Nelson at Saalbach.

She skied hard down the icy, technically difficult course and she won the race, her first World Cup victory since Grindelwald. This put her in the lead for the World Cup in downhill, the first time any American skier led the list in this demanding event.

By the time races resumed after the Christmas recess, Annemarie Moser-Proell had picked up steam again. At Grindelwald, the best and the worst of all races for Cindy, the downhill, was the next scheduled event. Unfavorable weather caused officials to change it to a giant slalom, which Annemarie won handily. Cindy could do no better than eighth, the best American showing.

No young skier was making her mark on the international ski scene as fast as Cindy Nelson was, and her popularity in the United States was really growing. When World Cup racing returned to North America after a year's interval, it gave the folks at home a chance to see Cindy and cheer her on. At Whistler Mountain, British Columbia, she won the first giant slalom race in her World Cup career.

At Jackson Hole, Wyoming, Cindy came in eighth in the season's last downhill. Her finish placed her fourth in the World Cup downhill standings for 1974-75, the best showing ever by an American.

**Cindy receiving her prize for giant slalom in Gari-
baldi, B.C. on the 1975 World Cup circuit.**

The highpoint of the 1975-76 ski season was, of course,
the Olympics at Innsbruck, Austria. Cindy and Lindy
Cochran were the only American women racers with any
significant world-class experience, and medal hopes rest-
ed with them. (In the absence of a previous Olympic
medalist on the U.S. team, Cindy had the honor of carry-
ing the American flag in the opening ceremony.)

The downhill is the only Olympic race where skiers actually get practice runs on the course before the event.
They attain such tremendous speeds in such a race that
it would be dangerous for them to ski all-out without
having tested the course first. In the slalom and giant
slalom, skiers inspect the course from the sidelines before each race.

Cindy's practice runs for her first Olympic race were not very encouraging. She fell or missed a gate in five of the eight runs she took. Her times to the halfway mark were good, but something was definitely wrong with her performance on the bottom half of the run.

Cindy and one of her coaches studied the course the day before the race and discovered that she had been veering almost ten feet away from the vertical line she should have been following in the bottom half of the run. Now she knew her mistake and wanted to do something about it, but she had no opportunity to practice again.

The weather on the day of the race was perfect, with a clear blue sky and comfortable sunshine by the time Cindy got to the starting gate, Rosi Mittermaier of West Germany was first in the competition. With an amazing time of 1:46.16, she had skied a perfect race. Brigitte Totschnig of Austria, who had been the pre-Olympics favorite, was second only by 83/100 of a second. There was little leeway for Cindy.

She exploded out of the starting gate with her usual burst of speed and barreled down the demanding course. She was concentrating so hard and going so fast that she couldn't hear the crowd chanting "Cindy! Cindy! Cindy!" as she shot by. She skied down the first steep section, made a sharp left and took the jump. Then she headed into the straightaway that led into another steep drop. At this point, she was skiing faster than most cars move on an expressway. She flew out of the straightaway and into the first S-turn between a stand of trees. Another turn and the finish line was in sight.

Cindy broke the electronic beam at the bottom of the course in 1:47.50, fast enough for a bronze medal if no one topped her performance. As she waited in the finish area fidgeting with a string of glass beads her sister had made for her, Cindy thought she would end up in fifth place. That wouldn't be bad, but it meant no medal. But no other racer bested her time. By taking third place, Cindy won the only Olympic medal in Alpine skiing for the United States in 1976.

As the 1976-77 racing season approached, it seemed as if Cindy would have a shot at becoming the first American World Cup winner. Rosi Mittermaier retired after winning three Olympic medals and her first World Cup in 10 years on the circuit. Rumors of Annemarie Moser-Proell's return were not being taken seriously because of her recent surgery.

Annemarie did return, but Cindy's excellent performances in early-season races gave her every reason to be confident about her World Cup chances. She finished in the top ten in races across the Alps—Val d'Isere, Courmayeur, Cortina d'Ampezzo and Zell am See. By Christmas, she had accumulated enough World Cup points to be solidly in sixth place.

Races resumed in January 1977 in Pfronten, the small German resort across the border from Austria. Annemarie won the 44th World Cup race of her career, while Cindy led the U.S. women with a disappointing 14th place in the downhill. When a reporter asked her what mistakes the American team was making, Cindy was annoyed but explained: "I don't think we made any particular mistakes. We just didn't ski fast enough."

Cindy was determined to rectify the situation at the next downhill which was scheduled for nearby Garmisch-Partenkirchen just four days later. Garmisch, a resort with a great skiing tradition, was the site of the 1936 Winter Olympics and would be the scene of the 1978 World Championships. To Cindy and every other international-class competitor, the races at Garmisch would be a dress rehearsal of sorts for the following year.

But Garmisch proved troublesome from the very first day. Forerunners, who ski a course to check it out before a race starts, found the last section of the downhill run extremely dangerous. The small finish line area was crisscrossed with ridges left by snow-grooming equipment. Skiers coming across them at very high speeds could easily take spills and become injured.

Of the first ten racers who took the downhill run, seven fell on the ridges. Cindy Nelson, who had logged a slightly improved 12th place, was one of the unlucky ones. She hit the bumps, tumbled hard, and slid into the protective hay bales which lined the finish area. As she slid, she slammed the tip of her left ski into a bale and snapped a bone in her left ankle.

Within three hours her ankle was in a cast and Cindy was on her way back home for surgery, rehabilitation, and a long wait before her next chance at the World Cup.

Cindy has always said that she'll keep racing as long as it pleases her. When she eventually does retire from competition, she wants to go to college. Her future plans include the development of a new ski resort or work in a field where she can use her knowledge of and interest in nature and wildlife. And maybe, if the women's pro circuit ever becomes a reality again, she might be lured into professional ski racing rather than retirement.

FOUR Racing for the Red, White, and Blue: Jana Hlavaty

Jana Hlavaty is, in many ways, the most remarkable skier on the U.S. cross-country ski team. She has made two comebacks and she skied her first Olympic race at an age when most athletes retire from amateur competition.

Jana Hlavaty was born in 1941 in Czechoslovakia. Twenty-one years later, while she was teaching literature and physical education in a mountain area in her country, she took up cross-country skiing. She liked it immediately and, within a few years, was representing Czechoslovakia in international competition. She enjoyed competing, not only because of the pleasure of the sport itself, but also because athletes from Communist countries could travel, an opportunity ordinary citizens do not have.

In 1968, Jana went to Chicago to spend her summer vacation with a recently widowed uncle. There, at a picnic, she met a young Czechoslovakian-born doctor named Vaclav Hlavaty. They were married three months later.

**Jana representing Czechoslovakia in Italy
during the 1966 Academic World Championship.**

Jana now had a new life as a wife and as a resident of
the United States. During the early months of her mar-
riage, she concentrated on learning English. Her husband
was putting in long hours at a nearby hospital, and she
used this time for English lessons. When she was speaking her new language fairly well, she began to think of
skiing. She wanted very much to take it up again, so she
began exercising to get herself back into physical shape.

But exercising was going to be a challenge in itself.
While most skiers live in country areas with plenty of
room to train, Jana lived in the city of Chicago. She had
to find ways to get around that situation if she was to get
herself ready. She began running up and down the stairs
of her 38-story apartment building. She also began intensive running on a nearby golf course, and she joined a lo-

cal health club. Jana needed to lift very heavy weights to strengthen her arms. The women's part of the club didn't have any that heavy, so she borrowed 150-pound weights from the men's gym. She even began to roller ski through Chicago's parks, to the surprise of lot of onlookers! She also was putting in daily hours of bicycle riding.

Jana's unusual conditioning program worked, because she was soon a candidate for the U.S. women's cross-country team.

Cross-country skiers are a breed apart from Alpine specialists. Their skis are lighter and thinner than Alpine skis, and the boots are cut low, similar to hiking shoes. The boot sole sticks out at the toe, and a binding clamps it to the ski. In contrast to Alpine equipment, the cross-country boot is flexible and the skier's heel is left free.

The motion cross-country skiers employ to propel themselves across the snow is a stride. Poles are used to help maintain both speed and stability. Special wax is applied to the ski bottoms which allows a sliding-forward motion but makes slide-back impossible.

A cross-country race course is several miles long and consists of uphill, downhill, and flat portions. The stamina required to compete is enormous. Experts in physical fitness have tested many kinds of athletes for their general conditioning. Cross-country skiers tend to be in better shape than most other athletes.

Skiers can practice on snow only about five months out of the year. In that time, American cross-country racers — both men and women — ski between 2,500 and 3,300 miles. The remaining seven months are spent working out on roller skis that look like elongated roller skates. Cross-country skiers also run, lift weights and bicycle to stay in shape. By the time the year has rolled around, the average U.S. world-class cross-country skier has logged something like 4,500 miles under his or her own body power.

The determination Jana applies to her training is one of her strongest assets. Her work toward increased stamina and strength is unending, and this is what has allowed her to stay in the running against skiers 10 or more years her junior.

Women's Olympic cross-country racing presently includes three events: the five-kilometer (about three miles), the 10-kilometer (about six miles), and the 4x5 relay, where each of four skiers does five kilometers. A 15-kilometer women's race will be in the 1980 Olympics. It is already part of many cross-country meets.

The difference between men and women racers' times is surprisingly small. Although the men ski longer races (up to 50 kilometers), their times are fairly close to the women's at various distances. While a top woman racer covers five kilometers in 15 minutes, men usually do it in 12½ minutes. The gap narrows as the distance grows. A world-class woman does the 10-kilometer course in 31 to 33 minutes which a man would ski in 29 or 30. Jana prefers longer distances and wishes there were more women's 20-kilometer races. She says you lose strength for the sprint as you grow older, but you don't lose endurance as long as you stay in shape.

Jana represented the United States in international competition for the first time in January 1973. She had to get State Department permission to do this, because she was not yet an American citizen. The race at Castelrotto Ronzone, Italy, was won by Martha Rockwell, the first American victory in four years in a European meet. Martha's time in the 7.5-kilometer race was 23.31.30, 30 seconds ahead of Michaela Endler of Germany. And right on Michaela's heels was Jana Hlavaty, skiing for the United States.

Other high placings followed that season, including an eighth place in the 10-kilometer event at the Holmenkollen, the most important cross-country race in Europe. Any placing in the top 25 is considered excellent in this race.

Jana started being a consistent runnerup to Martha Rockwell, America's best racer, starting at the 1973 U.S. Nationals and continuing through nearly every American race the following year. She won a rare victory over Martha at Michawye, Michigan, in 1974, making her the only U.S. racer to ever hand her teammate a defeat.

In international competition, however, neither Martha nor Jana were regarded as leaders. Russian and Finnish racers kept winning and winning and winning. Norway, Sweden, East Germany and Jana's native Czechoslovakia also boasted strong women's teams. When the U.S. State Department advised the U.S. Ski Association not to send Jana to race in East Germany for political reasons, she went on to the 1974 Holmenkollen, where she could do no better than 17th in the 10-kilometer race.

Jana did not compete during the 1974-75 season. Her husband's internship was over, and he was going to North Africa and the Middle East to research medical practices there. Jana chose to travel with him.

The 1976 Olympics were not totally out of her mind, however, and she continued training. She wrote home: "I ran in Istanbul, Beirut, Damascus, Jerusalem, Tel Aviv, Cairo, Tripoli, Tunis . . . I have run among bedouins, camels, donkeys and beggers in terrible poverty . . . I have run in mountains and on the sand dunes of the Sahara."

If Jana had caused a stir by roller-skiing in the parks of Chicago, it can only be imagined what the inhabitants

of these exotic cities thought as a long-legged blonde woman in a training suit puffed by.

When Jana and Vaclav returned to Chicago, she continued to train. She even found time in winter to visit
Seefeld, Austria, where the cross-country races of the
1976 Olympics were to be held. She had to stay in condition if she was to make her second comeback on the international racing scene.

U.S. ski officials wanted Jana on the 1976 Olympic
team, but there was one hitch. As 1975 drew to a close,
Jana was not yet an American citizen and therefore ineli-
gible to represent the U.S. in the Games. If everything
went according to regular procedure, Jana's citizenship
was due in March, a month after the Games were over.
The only way Jana could become part of the team was
by a special act of Congress.

Illinois Congressman Ralph H. Metcalfe, himself a former Olympic track team member, introduced a bill
which Senator Charles Percy helped steer through the
Senate. The bill was passed on December 16, 1975, and
sent to President Gerald Ford for signing.

Presidential aides told the Congressman and Senator
that the President was supposed to sign the bill before he
left for his own Christmas ski vacation at Vail, Colorado.
But somehow the bill got put aside. Every night, Jana
watched television news programs that showed the President skiing and relaxing.

"Please sign it!" Jana told the President on the television screen.

He finally put his signature on the bill the day before
New Year, and on January 5, 1976, Jana Hlavaty became
a citizen of the United States. Now she could compete for
America in the Winter Olympics. Getting on the Olympic
team was very important for her, both as an athlete and

**Signing her United States citizenship papers on the
eve of her departure for the Olympic Games.**

as a woman who settled here quite by accident and
learned what it is like to have a sense of political and
personal freedom.

The 1976 Winter Olympics were a bitter disappointment
for the women cross-country racers. Martha Rockwell
was just recovering from the flu and still suffering from
a previous ankle injury. Jana was considerably slowed
down by the start of a bad cold. Because Olympic officials were concerned that athletes might use illegal
drugs, they administered "doping tests" to the athletes
who took the highest placings in each event. Because of
these tests, team doctors would not prescribe medication
to anyone who was well enough to compete and had a
chance of doing well. So Jana Hlavaty's showings were

well down in the rankings because of the untreated cold.

Less than a month after the Games were over, Jana was back in top form. She swept all three women's events at the 1976 National Cross-Country Championships at Big Sky, Montana, edging out fellow Olympian Lynn VonderHeide by 7.23 seconds in the 10-kilometer race and defeating her by a strong 26.07 seconds in the five-kilometer race. She also trounced runnerup Joanne Musolf by nearly six minutes in the grueling 20-kilometer race.

Jana feels she has more drive now than she did when she was 20. She knows what she wants to do and she knows how to go about achieving her goals. She has trained her slender, long-limbed body to the peak of athletic strength and endurance. Dr. Art Dickinson, Nordic team trainer, has said that athletes who make demands on their bodies when they are in their 30s can accomplish anything they could when they were younger. They just have to work harder to maintain that condition.

Jana was again named to the U.S. Cross-Country Ski Team for the 1976-77 season. After considering it for a while, she decided to quit racing for good.

Now that Jana has retired, she has considered teaching physical education, as she did in Czechoslovakia. She believes Americans are not involved enough in sports and fitness.

Whenever an American teenager is old enough to drive, Jana says, he or she goes everywhere by car. Europeans tend to walk a great deal more than Americans, and walking in a small way contributes to overall fitness.

Jana would like to encourage American youngsters to train for sports and stay in shape. She knows the beauty of sports and would like to spend her life helping others realize it, too.

FIVE This New Thing Called Freestyle

Up to now, we've taken a look at modern versions of early forms of skiing. Today there is a new kind of ski competition called freestyle, similar in some ways to gymnastics, waterskiing, figure skating, and even daredevil auto racing!. A common nickname for freestyle skiing is hot dog skiing!

There are three kinds of freestyle: aerial, ballet and mogul. A freestyle competition consists of runs in all three events. Competitors are awarded points by a panel of judges for each of the runs.

In aerial events, competitors ski off a ramp or a jump built of snow—a similar kind of takeoff waterskiers use when they go off a ramp. While in the air they perform acrobatic maneuvers like somersaults, or spread-eagles, splits or other non-flipping moves.

Ballet competition is closest to figure skating. Skiers run down a smooth slope in time to music and perform various artistic moves on one or both skis. The moves are choreographed in advance and consist of both forward and backward skiing.

Mogul skiing is a fast-paced, exciting kind of freestyle. Competitors ski as quickly as they can down a steep, bumpy course (the bumps are known as moguls, which gives this event its name). Skiers go into the "valleys" between the bumps and over the tops of the bumps. Although they are in control of their skis, they make spectators think they are skiing with wild abandon. This is very similar to the impression you get when you watch highly skilled racing car drivers go through their paces.

Freestyle events stem from the experiments in the 1960's of a few skiers looking for new skills and horizons for their sport. Art Furrer, a Swiss-born ski school director in Vermont, started doing tricks similar to dance steps on skis to amuse himself. He bounced and wiggled down the slopes of Bolton Valley in time to music coming over the ski area's loudspeaker system. He was having fun, and visiting skiers enjoyed watching him.

Meanwhile, farther south at Sugarbush, Vermont, former Olympic gold medalist Stein Eriksen taught himself to do a somersault, or flip, in the air with skis on. Soon two young instructors at Killington, Vermont — Hermann Goellner and Tom LeRoi—worked on double and triple flips.

Moviemakers looking for new stunts to film in movies about skiing soon had Art, Tom, Hermann and others starring in a ski film each year, doing their acrobatic tricks, flips and other way-out moves. American sports fans were excited about this new free-form skiing, and by the late 1960's, young skiers were trying tricks on the slopes of mountains from coast to coast.

Skiing magazine's editor-in-chief Doug Pfeiffer traveled

across the country, saw what was happening, and predicted that freestyle was the wave of the future. He was instrumental in organizing the first major freestyle competition at Waterville Valley, New Hampshire, on March 5-6, 1971. It was a sensational success, and a new sport was born.

Waterville Valley prepared a single course for the event: one-third of it had big ramps for aerial takeoffs, one-third was filled with moguls, and the last third was smoothly groomed for ground tricks. The official name of the competition was the National Championship of Exhibition Skiing, but that was too formal a title for the circus-on-skis that actually took place. It was really a bunch of good skiers doing their own thing on the snow, with few rules, if any, to follow!

Competitors tried all kinds of stunts. Two skiers even performed together on one pair of skis! The "old pros" of the new sport were there, too, led by Hermann Goellner who flipped his way to winning the top prize, a Corvette.

One person stood out among all the competitors—Suzy Chaffee, the only woman who was competing. Tall, blonde, and a dazzling beauty, she was remarkably good at freestyle. She had been a member of the 1968 Olympic team and was the best American downhiller of her day. Now she was a successful magazine and television model.

Suzy was a striking figure in her bright red, one-piece ski suit. Her graceful performance in trick (or ballet) skiing enable her to score higher than the mountain full of men she was competing against. But Suzy brought more than style and form to freestyle. From that very first event, she became the spokeswoman for all women freestylers and she worked hard to get them every benefit that male competitors enjoyed. One change that Suzy is responsible for is guaranteeing that every five-judge freestyle panel have at least one woman member. That change did not come fast or easy.

The next freestyle competition was six weeks later at Vail, Colorado. Separate courses were laid out for mogul, ballet, and aerial events, and each skier had to compete in all three. There was still no woman judge, but Suzy, who tied for third in the ballet event, kept plugging for her idea.

During the 1971-72 season, three major freestyle competitions—sponsored by **Skiing** magazine and Chevrolet — took place. Thanks to Suzy, women judges were on all panels, and she was no longer the only woman competitor. She and a talented skier named Pat Karnik both placed in the top three in the ballet event.

It is important to remember that the first women freestylers competed against the men, skied the same slopes, and were judged by the same judges. This is different from ski racing. While women are able to hold their own in the ballet event, they don't have the physical strength to keep up with the men's pace in the mogul run. Women in early freestyle events didn't attempt flips like the men were doing, and this made their aerials less spectacular to watch. Under these circumstances, women had virtually no chance of winning big in freestyle.

Led by Suzy Chaffee, the growing ranks of female freestylers began asking for a separate women's circuit. Suzy also started asking serious questions about safety and control in freestyle skiing before the 1973 events started. She wondered why hot dogging had developed into a daredevil contest. She wanted to know why skiers were rewarded by judges for the most dangerous flips and wildest mogul runs. She wanted to know why skiers were trying to impress judges with nerve rather than

skill, and why strength was valued more than grace.

"Male judges instinctively reinforce those who ski powerfully and aggressively," Suzy explained. "The way the game is stacked against women skiers now, women just can't afford economically and psychologically to show up."

By this she meant that if a woman could not possibly win a share of the prize money, it would be a waste to lay out the expenses, travel money, and the $25 entry fee for each competition without hope of winning it back. Also, women found it discouraging to keep competing, knowing defeat was all that was in store for them.

But freestyle was growing. A second major tour was established called the Super Hot Dog competitions; it was sponsored by a ski-importer called Beconta and by **Ski** magazine. Series of small tours were held in different parts of the country, too. More and more women were getting involved in freestyle competition.

In the midst of this growth, however, two tragic accidents in the spring of 1973 made organizers of freestyle competitions remember Suzy Chaffee's concern about safety. Two young men tried to do multiple-revolution back flips. Both failed, broke their spines, and will be totally paralyzed for the rest of their lives.

After the accidents the International Freestyle Skiers Association was formed. This was an organization of free-stylers who policed themselves. A committee of leading competitors was formed to determine each competitor's qualification to do complicated moves, especially aerials where all serious injuries to date had occurred. In line with Suzy's idea only single-revolution flips were allowed at IFSA-sanctioned events.

Suzy Chaffee   **Genia Fuller**

Another of Suzy Chaffee's suggestions was adopted at the Sun Valley championships, the last event in the spring of 1973: a separate women's prize structure was established. It surprised no one when Suzy, the veteran, took first place. Women's prizes at Sun Valley totalled $1,000, but that came nowhere near the total cash value of the men's prizes. The top men's prize alone — a car — was worth at least $5,000. The women complained, and IFSA soon decided they had a point. The association recommended that women be eligible to compete for special prize money in addition to, not instead of, the main purse in each competition. It was suggested that 14.25 per cent of the prizes be reserved for women.

IFSA's reasoning went like this. The association was banning double and triple flips and allowing each competitor just one single-revolution flip in each aerial competition. IFSA felt that women competed equally with men in the ballet event and now in the aerials. The association felt that the 14.25 per cent bonus compensated for the disadvantage women still had in the mogul event. IFSA's offer was a step in the right direction.

Suzy Chaffee was no longer a lone female voice in a chorus of male freestylers. As more women entered the competitions, they were anxious for bigger stakes. So, late in 1973, the World Hot Dog Association was formed to obtain sponsorship for a women's freestyle tour. Many female skiers expected to belong to both WHSA and IFSA, which still welcomed women to compete in its events.

The first competition of 1974 was again at Waterville Valley. With special women's prize money at stake, something unusual happened. The top woman actually skied off with more money that weekend than the top man. Genia Fuller, a former figure skater, placed first in all three events, a feat achieved by no man. Her win-

Ellen Post

Marion Post

nings totaled $950. The top male winner, Bob Salerno, earned $600. He took home a car too, but the women were satisfied with the year's progress in their battle for recognition.

The second big competition of the season was the World Super Hot Dog Championship, sponsored by Beconta and offering a total of $35,000 in prize money. Men and women competed for the same purse, but there was a new twist to the rules. Of nearly 200 skiers seeking to qualify for 60 starting numbers, 20 were women.

So the Beconta people decided women "owned" 10 per cent of the entry field. Therefore, of the 60 starters, six would be women. At the first cut, the field would be narrowed to 40, four of them women. And finally, of the 20 skiers in the final running of each event — aerial, ballet, and mogul — the top 18 men and two women would be included.

Skiing against 180 men, Genia Fuller turned in a fine performance that netted her an overall ninth place. Her ballet run was spectacular in spite of a painfully bruised shoulder, and she turned in a fast, exciting mogul run that proved a woman **could** be strong, athletic, and yet graceful on a demanding course.

Finally on April 6-7, 1974, at Copper Mountain, Colorado, a milestone was achieved by women freestylers. Top female competitors in the U.S. got a chance to hold their own meet with $10,000 in prize money put up by Budweiser. The judges were looking for grace and control, and no aerials were included.

Marion Post, half of a twin-sister duo of freestylers, won the ballet as the cheers of a crowd of spectators accompanied her down the slope. Shorter than most freestylers, Marion has become famous for extremely demanding ballet runs to make up for her lack of height.

The mogul competition was held on Pitch, a steep, bumpy run which is a breathtaking 11,900 feet above sea level. The altitude made the tricky course even tougher. The winner was 24-year-old Julie Meissner from the high country of Bend, Oregon, where ski racers train in summer. She skipped down the fall line skimming the bumps in perfect control. The crowd cheered wildly for this newcomer to bigtime freestyle. Women freestylers proved they could turn on an audience, which was important for them all.

Throughout the rest of the winter of 1974, Genia Fuller established herself as a star on the freestyle circuit. She was the first competitor, male or female, to win the overall, mogul, ballet, and aerial titles at one event, and she has been called the Woman Freestyler of the Year both by **Skiing** magazine and **Ski Racing**, a newspaper which covers ski competitions of all kinds.

While Suzy Chaffee was an activist for all women skiers, Genia (whose name is pronounced Gain-yuh) sought commercial sponsorship among ski equipment and clothing manufacturers as top male freestylers had done. She showed companies that it is good business to promote their goods through a woman competitor. Today more and more sportswomen are being signed up by manufacturers for product promotion.

Originally from Framingham, Massachusetts, a suburb of Boston, Genia was a competitive figure skater for 11 years. She started skiing at the age of 12 and is a certified ski instructor and freestyle ski coach. Her skating gave her the quick footwork and rhythm for ballet skiing, as well as the balance and strength that makes her such a fine mogul skier. In addition, she is an excellent aerialist and was one of the first women to do flips in freestyle competition.

What made Genia especially appealing to sponsors were her wholesome all-American looks and her outgoing personality. Genia has long brown hair and a dimpled smile. When she gets ready to ski, she acts calm and looks as if she's really relaxed and having fun. But beneath that placid exterior is a competitive athlete whose consistently strong placings have won her the respect of other freestylers.

The changes in freestyle competition from 1971 to 1974 were amazing, and they changed the lives of freestyle skiers very dramatically. In the early days of the event, skiers would show up on the weekend of a meet and ski as well as they could for the prizes offered. In summer, they took jobs to keep them going till the snow fell again.

By the mid-'70s, competitions had become highly formalized. IFSA, although weakening as an organization, had set up standards for competition organizers and competitors themselves. Serious injuries were no longer a problem. Ballet skiers added music to their choreographed routines. And skiers began training year-round and attending, or teaching at, freestyle camps, much as racers had been doing for years.

At the beginning of the 1974-75 ski season, women freestylers finally made it big. Colgate-Palmolive came up with $90,000 to sponsor a televised women's freestyle program. Budweiser also decided on a $54,000 women's tour. The combination looked especially good in a year when IFSA's internal problems were growing. The combined Budweiser and Colgate purses amount to more than six times what the women had been given the year before as a share of the general prize money.

Meanwhile, the Professional Freestyle Associates spun off from IFSA. PFA decided each of its competitions would consist of an elite group of 40 men and 15 women. Female freestylers were getting to be "hot" property in the world of hot dog skiing. Those skiing women who had worked so hard were optimistic about their future in the world of professional athletics.

The first meet of the 1974-75 winter was at Aspen, Colorado, with blowing snow and near-zero visibility stretching the schedule beyond the two days originally planned. Genia Fuller strung together a fourth in the ballet and second place in the aerials and moguls for a first place in the combined. This was pretty much where she had left off in her successful previous season.

Second places in the moguls and ballet plus a third in the aerials in the next freestyle meet on the Colgate tour brought Genia another first place at Stowe, Vermont, a few months later. And a few weeks after that, she put together her third combined triumph at Park City West, Utah. That was where Genia was living at the time, and the home crowd was out in force to cheer their champ. Genia Fuller was beginning to look unbeatable.

The event the women were really proud of was the $20,000 Women's Ballet-Freestyle World Championships held in Park City, Utah, on March 15-17, 1975. The championships were all theirs; they did not have to share the limelight with the men. It felt good to have something that was by and for women skiers, and they were determined to make it good.

The women decided to try dual-format mogul skiing. Two skiers would be on the course at the same time, skiing against each other as well as for points. This would make it a faster, more exciting spectator event.

The format is used successfully in professional ski racing, so the women wanted to give it a try in freestyle. It worked so well that some men's events have been patterned after it ever since.

Judy Nagel, a veteran racer who had been on the 1968 Olympic team with Suzy Chaffee, proved to be a natural freestyler. After placing second at the women's freestyle meet at Copper Mountain her first time out, Judy really poured it on, besting other ex-racers and experienced mogul competitors in a near-perfect performance.

Another newcomer named Wendy Von Allmen won the $2,400 first place in the ballet event in a field of 28 women that did not include Fuller, Chaffee, and other big guns of women's freestyle. They could not compete at Park City, because they were off at Crested Butte, Colorado, at a coed meet.

Genia Fuller won nearly $21,000 for the season and captured the 1975 Freestyle Competitor of the Year award for the second year in a row. By the age of 20, she had put together a spectacular ski career. In fact, Genia and Suzy have been able to turn their skiing into dollars more successfully than any other women on the slopes.

The 1975-76 ski season dawned with heady prospects for freestylers, not the least of which was nearly half a million dollars in promised purses. Professional Freestyle Associates had become the sport's prime governing body, with most of the big names under exclusive contract. PFA also gave its competitions a new name, the 1976 PFA World Trophy Freestyle Tour.

A second tour, for men, was also established. Known as the Chevrolet American Freestyle Skiing Tour, it allowed women to enter and compete against the men, event for event, as in the early days. This was an unfortunate step backward in freestyle competition.

In addition, the second Budweiser Women's Ballet-Mogul Championships was scheduled at Vail, Colorado, in March. It was the first freestyle event at Vail since 1973, and it demonstrated Vail's confidence that the women would put on a safe contest.

Genia Fuller continued her winning ways in PFA meets in 1975-76, placing high in almost all individual events and coming in first in the combined standings at Heavenly Valley and Stratton Mountain, Vermont, where she had moved to teach freestyle at Stratton Academy.

Marion and Ellen Post, Karen Huntoon and former U.S. Ski Team racers Sandra Poulsen and Susie Corrock were among the skiers nipping at Genia's ski tails.

For the first time, women's freestyle events were held in Europe under the PFA organization.

Marion Post wound up the 1976 freestyle season in first place, topping Genia Fuller who was out of the last three meets because of surgery. Marion ended the season with a spectacular first place in both the ballet and moguls at the final PFA competition at Snowbird, Utah. Her season winnings amounted to $29,205. The top male competitor, Scott Brooksbank, won $21,180. This made Marion Post the first professional woman athlete to earn more prize money in a season than the top man in the same sport.

As had happened so often in its brief history, freestyle's 1976-77 season opened with uncertainty. Organizers of the Chevrolet Freestyle tour were embroiled in a lawsuit with PFA, which didn't firm up its own schedule and sponsors until after the season's first snowfall.

When the season finally got underway, it was a brief one for the women, who had only three competitions to enter. But there was big money at stake, money that equalled the men's purses.

Genia Fuller was fit and back on the tour, going head to head with Marion Post for the overall freestyle title, now called the World Trophy Championship, which both had held.

The first competition was at Stratton Mountain, Vermont, and Marion Post took the combined first place. Genia Fuller tied for second right behind her. The second competition of the season was a non-PFA, women-only event consisting just of ballet and mogul competitions at Winter Park, Colorado. Marion Post again ran away with first place in the ballet and a hefty chunk of the $25,000 in prize money put up by Budweiser, while Genia Fuller took sixth place. Neither woman qualified in the moguls, which not surprisingly was dominated by former racers. However, this was not serious in terms of the World Trophy standings, since it was not included there.

Heavenly Valley, California—one of the original and certainly one of the longest-running sites for freestyle competitions—was the scene of the 1977 Easter weekend women's freestyle events. Marion Post took first place in both the ballet and the aerials, which more than compensated for her eighth place finish in the mogul run. While ex-champ Genia Fuller only placed fifth the overall, Marion took the overall title and retained her position as the top woman freestyle skier in the world for the second year in a row.

In just six years, freestyle skiing in general went from small potatoes to the big time.

Women on skis **can** be "good box office" as they say in show business.

ABOUT THE AUTHOR

Claire Walter is a former managing editor of **SKI** and has also contributed articles to **womenSports** and **Ski Racing** magazines. She attended the 1976 Winter Olympic Games as well as World Cup and U.S. ski competitions. Claire now lives in New Jersey. She is on the Board of Directors of the Eastern Ski Writers Association.